WORLD WAR III

WORLD WAR III

God's Conquest of Russia

by
Hilton Sutton

HARRISON HOUSE
Tulsa, Oklahoma

WORLD WAR III
ISBN 0-89274-192-9
Copyright © 1982 by Hilton Sutton
Mission To America
736 Wilson Road
Humble, Texas 77338

Published by Harrison House, Inc.
P. O. Box 35035
Tulsa, Oklahoma 74135

Contents

Foreword

The Unfolding of a Great Event in the Plan of God

Bible prophecy has come into its own since the Reunification of Jerusalem in 1967. From that time until Jesus appears in the air for His Church, we must be informed of what comes next in the plan of God.

On three separate occasions I have sat spellbound as Hilton Sutton, the prophecy preacher, has shared ''God's Conquest of Russia.'' Many have requested that this message be placed in print for all to enjoy.

In this fourth edition, a word picture of the actual battle soon to take place in the mountains of Judea is set forth in such a fashion that you are there in the thick of the battle. I know that many will be blessed as they read the unfolding of one of the great events to take place in the plan of God.

Charles Rogers
Director, Evangelism In Action

Introduction

Many live today as though there were no tomorrow. A vast lack of knowledge concerning the future is the reason for such behavior.

The question, then, is: "How can we know the future?"

My answer: by **knowing** what the Holy Scriptures have to say! Several times in the Scriptures we are told that we should not be ignorant of the things to come.

The subject matter of this book is not necessarily light, but it does give us insight into the immediate future. Especially, it informs us of coming events that parallel the appearing of our Lord Jesus Christ.

God's Conquest of Russia

In setting forth the story of *World War III — God's Conquest of Russia*, I am actually setting the stage for the appearing of Jesus and the blessed "catching up" of the Church. *These two events are almost simultaneous.*

As the story unfolds, one becomes aware that this major event, World War III, follows the catching up of the Church in a very quick sequence. Many of the biblical signs that point to the appearing of Jesus and the catching up of the Church also set the stage for this story, so vividly set forth in chapters 38 and 39 of Ezekiel. The prophecies of the Old Testament and the words of Jesus, concerning the restoration of Israel in the end time, point directly to both events.

Jesus Is Coming

This book is the story of World War III which is not the battle of Armageddon. An explanation of the two separate events is contained in this book.

I ask that you read this book prayerfully, then share this scriptural revelation with many others. *Time is short; Jesus is coming!* It is clear in the Scriptures that we are not to know the day nor the hour of His appearing, but of the season of His appearing we are not to be ignorant. Without question we are in the period of time in which the appearing of Christ will occur!

I dedicate this work to those who search for the truth that shall make them free.

God's Conquest of Russia in Scripture

Words that abundantly support the content of this book, the biblical account from the prophet Ezekiel:

Chapter 38

1 And the word of the Lord came unto me, saying,

2 Son of man, set thy face against Gog, the land of Magog, the chief prince of Meshech and Tubal, and prophesy against him,

3 And say, Thus saith the Lord God; Behold, I am against thee, O Gog, the chief prince of Meshech and Tubal:

4 And I will turn thee back, and put hooks into thy jaws, and I will bring thee forth, and all thine army, horses and horsemen, all of them clothed with all sorts of armour, even a great company with bucklers and shields, all of them handling swords:

5 Persia, Ethiopia, and Libya with them; all of them with shield and helmet:

6 Gomer, and all his bands; the house of Togarmah of the north quarters, and all his bands: and many people with thee.

7 Be thou prepared, and prepare for thyself, thou, and all thy company that are assembled unto thee, and be thou a guard unto them.

8 After many days thou shalt be visited: in the latter years thou shalt come into the land that is brought back from the sword, and is gathered out of many people, against the mountains of Israel, which have been always waste: but it is brought forth out of the nations, and they shall dwell safely all of them.

9 Thou shalt ascend and come like a storm, thou shalt be like a cloud to cover the land, thou, and all thy bands, and many people with thee.

10 Thus saith the Lord God; It shall also come to pass, that at the same time shall things come into thy mind, and thou shalt think an evil thought:

11 And thou shalt say, I will go up to the land of unwalled villages; I will go to them that are at rest, that dwell safely, all of them dwelling without walls, and having neither bars nor gates,

12 To take a spoil, and to take a prey; to turn thine hand upon the desolate places that are now inhabited, and upon the people that are gathered out

of the nations, which have gotten cattle and goods, that dwell in the midst of the land.

13 Sheba, and Dedan, and the merchants of Tarshish, with all the young lions thereof, shall say unto thee, Art thou come to take a spoil? hast thou gathered thy company to take a prey? to carry away silver and gold, to take away cattle and goods, to take a great spoil?

14 Therefore, son of man, prophesy and say unto Gog, Thus saith the Lord God; In that day when my people of Israel dwelleth safely, shalt thou not know it?

15 And thou shalt come from thy place out of the north parts, thou, and many people with thee, all of them riding upon horses, a great company, and a mighty army:

16 And thou shalt come up against my people of Israel, as a cloud to cover the land; it shall be in the latter days, and I will bring thee against my land, that the heathen may know me, when I shall be sanctified in thee, O Gog, before their eyes.

17 Thus saith the Lord God; Art thou he of whom I have spoken in old time by my servants the prophets of Israel, which prophesied in those days many years that I would bring thee against them?

18 And it shall come to pass at the same time when Gog shall come against the land of Israel, saith the Lord God, that my fury shall come up in my face.

19   For in my jealousy and in the fire of my wrath have I spoken, Surely in that day there shall be a great shaking in the land of Israel;

20   So that the fishes of the sea, and the fowls of the heaven, and the beasts of the field, and all creeping things that creep upon the earth, and all the men that are upon the face of the earth, shall shake at my presence, and the mountains shall be thrown down, and the steep places shall fall, and every wall shall fall to the ground.

21   And I will call for a sword against him throughout all my mountains, saith the Lord God: every man's sword shall be against his brother.

22 And I will plead against him with pestilence and with blood; and I will rain upon him, and upon his bands, and upon the many people that are with him, an overflowing rain, and great hailstones, fire, and brimstone.

23 Thus will I magnify myself, and sanctify myself; and I will be known in the eyes of many nations, and they shall know that I am the Lord.

Chapter 39

1 Therefore, thou son of man, prophesy against Gog, and say, Thus saith the Lord God; Behold, I am against thee, O Gog, the chief prince of Meshech and Tubal:

2 And I will turn thee back, and leave but the sixth part of thee, and will cause thee to come up from the north parts, and will bring thee upon the mountains of Israel:

3 And I will smite thy bow out of thy left hand, and will cause thine arrows to fall out of thy right hand.

4 Thou shalt fall upon the mountains of Israel, thou, and all thy bands, and the people that is with thee: I will give thee unto the ravenous birds of every sort, and to the beasts of the field to be devoured.

5 Thou shalt fall upon the open field: for I have spoken it, saith the Lord God.

6 And I will send a fire on Magog, and among them that dwell carelessly in the isles: and they shall know that I am the Lord.

7 So will I make my holy name known in the midst of my people Israel; and I will not let them pollute my holy name any more: and the heathen shall know that I am the Lord, the Holy One in Israel.

8 Behold, it is come, and it is done, saith the Lord God; this is the day whereof I have spoken.

9 And they that dwell in the cities of Israel shall go forth, and shall set on fire and burn the weapons, both the shields and the bucklers, the bows and the arrows, and the handstaves, and the spears, and they shall burn them with fire seven years:

10 So that they shall take no wood out of the field, neither cut down any out of the forests; for they shall burn the weapons with fire: and they shall spoil those that spoiled them, and rob those that robbed them, saith the Lord God.

Events in the Final Drama

Involving Russia, Israel, Mankind, Earth, and the Second Coming of Jesus Christ:

1917 Bolshevik Revolution, czar overthrown

1917 to
1940 Internal unrest

1940 Alliance with Axis power

1941 War with Germany

1945 War ends

1946 Russia gets eastern Europe

1946 to
1955 "Peaceable Coexistence," Communism and Capitalism

1956 Russia crushes Hungarian Freedom Fighters

1956 Russia drawn militarily into Middle East over Suez Canal event

1957	Russia launched first Sputnik satellite
1960	Russia shoots down U.S. spy plane; destroys Summit Conference
1967	Russia, with best military strategy and equipment, defeated by Israel in Six-Day War
1968	Russia crushes Czechoslovakian uprising
1969	Russia backs North Vietnamese
1973	Russia backs Arabs for Yom Kippur War
1973	Detente
1975	Russia becomes number 1 militarily by reason of numerical strength
1976	Russia's serious trouble: agricultural failures, social upheaval, nature's unheaval, threatened by China

Russia's
Prophesied
Future   Russia will attempt to swallow up Middle East, but Israel will stand in the way

1
God's Conquest of Russia

1
God's Conquest of Russia

The setting for this study is found in chapters 38 and 39 of Ezekiel in which the prophet Ezekiel received specific instructions from the Lord to speak forth a prophecy concerning a particular geographical area. This prophecy involves the present nation of Russia, her allies, and the nation of Israel.

Ezekiel is always very quick to identify his source of information.

And the word of the Lord came unto me, saying, Son of man, set thy face against Gog, the land of Magog, the chief prince of Meshech and Tubal, and prophesy against him,

And say, Thus saith the Lord God; Behold, I am against thee, O Gog, the chief prince of Meshech and Tubal.

Ezekiel 38:1-3

Ezekiel speaks concerning a specific geographical area of the earth. His prophecy to that area, its people and its leaders, refers to the same geographical locations that now include the nation of Russia.

On old biblical maps, the territories of Gog and Magog and the provinces of Meshech and Tubal are all found within the confines of the geographical region known today as Russia. As this chapter continues, other provinces will be mentioned that are also found within the same geographical location.

"Behold, I Am Against Thee"

In verse 3 Ezekiel speaks the words of God, declaring, *Behold, I am against thee, O Gog, the chief prince of Meshech and Tubal.* Whenever God says, "I am against you," you can be certain that you are in trouble — very serious trouble.

There are not many occasions in the Scriptures in which God so directly says He is against a certain person, people, or geographical area. When He reaches the place where He has been long in patience, having pled, called, and withheld His wrath to prevent the destruction of people, but still they repent not, He is left with no alternative except to allow them to destroy themselves. Should they attempt in their rebellion to harm His people, He will intervene, and do so with great fury.

The Word of God bears me out in this account again and again. As long as Israel sought the Lord, He stood by them and delivered them. He would step in and make up the difference for them, giving them surpassing victories over insurmountable odds. They were never defeated except at times of disobedience when they turned away from God. We have the established record of the Word of God that He will not suffer His own to be defeated or destroyed, but instead will destroy the destroyer — Satan.

Allow me to join Ezekiel in clearly saying that God is against the land of Russia and its leadership. The land of Magog, headed up by Gog, the chief prince of Meshech and Tubal, is an exact description of Russia. I emphasize, Russia is in trouble!

How can we identify this Gog and Magog? First of all, let me say this is not the Gog and Magog of Revelation, chapter 20. The Gog and Magog of Revelation, chapter 20, identifies followers of Satan, which he gathers from all over the earth at the end of the 1,000-year reign of Christ upon the earth. Both Russia and that particular following of Satan are identified as Gog and Magog, so we can easily say the terms *Gog* and *Magog* are used to identify godless people.

The Gog and Magog of Ezekiel 38 is a fixed geographical area and a specific people, not a large company of people from all over the earth as is the case with the Magog crowd of Revelation 20. Magog of Ezekiel 38 and 39 is the second son of Japheth, the son of Noah. In other words, Magog is the grandson of Noah. The descendants of Magog settled in a vast area of northern Europe and Asia known as Scythia.

Other names mentioned in this reference help us to identify the area. The vast ancient area of Scythia lies completely within the geographical boundaries of the Soviet Union. Persia (Iraq and Iran), Ethiopia, Libya, Gomer (eastern Europe), and Togarmah (Turkey) are being swallowed up by the Soviet Union. (vv. 5,6.)

The province of Meshech included the geographical location of the present city of Moscow. In the province of Tubal there now exists the Russian city of Tobolsk. Togarmah's descendants were to occupy the southern part of the nation we know as Russia, along with Rumania, Bulgaria, and Turkey. The geographical area that we know as eastern Europe — East Germany, Poland, Hungary, and Czechoslovakia — was originally settled by the descendants of Gomer.

The use of modern names to identify nations does no damage to the scriptural account.

The prophecy of Ezekiel 38 is totally dependent upon the existing state of Israel. At the time Ezekiel was setting forth these things, most of Israel was already in captivity and the captivity was soon to be completed. There was no state of Israel from that time until May of 1948. The stage was then set for this very prophecy to begin to unfold and come to pass.

My friend, today you are watching the greatest performance the world has ever known. It ought to excite you as you have never been excited before!

A few months ago, someone asked me, "Hilton, do you always write on prophecy?"

"Always," I said, "unless the Lord directs me otherwise."

"Doesn't that get a little boring?" My answer was simple: "Indeed not!"

Prophecy allows the Bible student to literally observe God keeping His Word. A study of the prophetic Scriptures is like having the program of a grand play, allowing you to accurately follow along act after act. A master performance of God is unfolding by the day. Act after act is being staged, leading to the grand finale. All nations are included and the whole story is excitingly dramatic.

More than twenty-six hundred years ago, God spoke through Ezekiel and predicted the rise of Russia and its threat to the new nation of Israel.

As surely as there was handwriting on the wall in the time of Belshazzar, Emperor of Babylon, there is handwriting on the walls of the Kremlin in Moscow. The present leaders in

Russia know they are in trouble, but they are at a loss to know how to handle their dilemma. They are left with no alternative: They must resort to the use of force, which of course will lead to their destruction.

Russia is in trouble. She is set up like the ten pins on a bowling alley. Everything is in order now for God to say, "I've waited as long as I'm going to wait. I'm going to release judgment and wrath upon the nation that has said, 'I will come like a storm. I will be like a cloud covering the land of Israel. I will sweep in against the unprotected cities of Israel and gather up their cattle and goods as a spoil." (vv. 9-12.)

Russia Needs The Mid-East

Why must Russia have the Middle East? There are several distinct reasons.

First, the Middle East happens to be the most strategic military spot on earth. The Middle East is the key geographical area that links Asia to both

Europe and Africa. When in control of that area, a nation is sitting in a key military position.

Secondly, Russia needs the vast supply of untapped natural resources that are housed in the Middle East. Israel is a fabulous food basket—and Russia needs food! Ezekiel 38:12 predicts that Russia will come against Israel for food. When she does, God will stand against her in defense of His people. (Ezek. 38:18-23.)

Thirdly, Russia needs the Middle East in order to alleviate herself from the internal pressures of having two major military fronts, one on the west and one on the east. The Russians fear having to fight on two major fronts. Russians do not respond well to pressure. Their self-confidence is not the best in the world and Russian morale is not very stable.

The best morale and self-confidence in the world ranks evenly between the United States and Israel. Russia is trying to erode away some of the western European defense and weaken that position.

2
Russia vs. China

2
Russia vs. China

According to the news media, Russia no longer considers the United States her only opponent. China has now become her enemy. Alternately, China no longer considers the United States her number one adversary. Russia has taken the position as China's foremost enemy.

You may ask, "Do you believe that God has charted the courses of these two anti-God nations so that perhaps they will destroy one another?"

My answer must be, "No."

Both Russia and China are geared for world conquest. As far as political and military science is concerned, they are on a collision course. However, they will never collide. Such an event is not in the plan of God. The prophetic Scriptures do not reveal it.

Remember, God is a stickler for divine order. He designed His plan and He will not deviate from it. It is His will that none should perish; however, He will allow to be destroyed those that oppose Him and attempt to destroy His people.

There will never be a major military confrontation between Russia and China. Both will have their "Waterloos," but these "Waterloos" will be separated by a period of seven years.

Russia's defeat comes at the very beginning of the Tribulation Period within what could be only hours of the appearing of Jesus and the catching away of the Church to meet Him in the air.

China's military forces, after great success in the Orient and in Asia, are to

36

arrive at the back door of Israel. They will cross the dried-up River Euphrates, turn south into the state of Israel, and arrive at the battle site of Armageddon, where they will meet their "Waterloo." Within one hour China and ten other massive European and Mediterranean armies will be dissolved into a pool of blood that covers an area of 200 miles. (See Rev. 14.)

Again, I emphasize that Russia is in serious trouble today. She must have the Middle East open to her. This will provide a waterway through which she can move very quickly into Asian and Oriental waters and confront China on two sides with nuclear warheads, thus neutralizing the threat of China.

If Russia could successfully gain control of the Mid-East and place a powerful naval force off the China coast, China would be in trouble. That would almost eliminate Russia's eastern front. Of course, she will not succeed.

3
Troubles in Russia

3
Troubles in Russia

Russia is in trouble externally, militarily, and internally. The pressure is building toward the time in which she will make that fatal mistake of attempting to invade Israel. Ezekiel describes the attack as a storm coming to cover the land. Why Israel? Because Israel is the only force keeping Russia out of the Middle East right now. If it had not been for Israel, Russia would already be there. The Arabs with their lack of unity would be no opposition for her. Israel is the thorn in Russia's side.

Russia is in trouble internally. Among other things, she lacks heavy industry. In 1973 Leonid Brezhnev, General Secretary of the Communist party in the Soviet Union, came to the United States for a week. He had a number of sessions with President Nixon and also with a group of American businessmen.

Why did Brezhnev meet with American industrialists — men known in Russia as capitalists? To gain help with Russia's serious shortage of heavy industry. He wanted to know how the people of his nation could upgrade their living standards. To do this, he needed American capitalists to make large investments in Russia and build heavy industry to meet the needs of the Russian people. That certainly was a switch!

Surely we were not foolish enough to meet Brezhnev's request. Well, partially. You might say, then, that we Americans are dumb. Keep reading and you may not think so.

Why does Russia suddenly have such a need for industrial development? Because of her serious internal problems.

As hard as the Communists have worked to keep the Western influence out of Russia, it has still crept in. With America being the most copied nation on earth, Russia has joined the crowd, at least to some extent.

If an American visits Russia today, there are various things he will be permitted to see. He will be taken to Moscow and shown the little they have of what America has in abundance, such as supermarkets and department stores.

As the American walks through one of these supermarkets, observing the rows of shelves, his Russian guide will say, "See what we are doing for our people! Like you Americans, we have fine supermarkets. Our shelves are one-third filled."

The American will look at them and probably think, *No, they are two-thirds empty*.

Because of Western influence, the Russian people have begun to put pressure on the Kremlin. Department stores now appear in major Russian cities. However, of all the items on display, there may be only a few dozen of each and the price is prohibitive. Shirts, ties, suits, dresses, coats, shoes — all are in short supply. But, nevertheless, they do have department stores.

The Russian people are beginning to ask for items which to them are luxuries, but to Americans these items are a part of their everyday lives — items such as telephones, radios, TV's. In America we are surrounded with telephones, while most Russian families would like to have just one. The Russian people are craving television, even though few families are financially able to afford them. We in America are plagued by radio and television. Often there are two or three of each in our homes, not to mention our offices, automobiles, and airplanes.

Automobiles are another desire of the Russian people. The average

American home today looks like a used-car lot. When only a few years ago, there was only one family car to each home, today we have two family cars, a hot rod, a pickup, a Honda, and four bicycles!

I am not writing this to be humorous, but to point out the things America has that the Russian people are beginning to want. Western influence has penetrated behind the Iron Curtain and the Russians are beginning to come alive. They are beginning to realize that they can have a higher standard of living — and they want it!

This realization is bringing pressure on the Kremlin. The Kremlin doesn't dare ignore the people and add to its internal problems. Its two great external problems are enough!

But Russia's internal problems go further. There is a democratic movement on the rise that is much stronger than the Russians will permit the Western world to know. This movement has become so strong inside Russia that some of its outstanding leaders have been either deported or imprisoned.

Part of this internal problem stems from the fact that the Bolshevik Revolution which occurred in 1917 has never ended. The Communists would have the world to believe that they won their revolution — that they are in absolute control of Russia. However, since 1917 these Communists have put to death more than 66 million Russians to reach the place they hold in this hour. Today some 250 million Russians are slaves to only about 30 million hard-core Communists.

This information should have appeared on the front page of every American newspaper instead of as a small article near the back of the main news section. I can't understand why the news media continues to try to protect Communism and Russia.

Russia's troubles continue to increase. Industrially and socially, she is underdeveloped. Militarily, she is getting in over her head. Agriculturally, she is in trouble. Over the past sixteen growing seasons, Russia has experienced thirteen crop failures. While some were small, others were immense. The 1981 crop failure was one of the worst.

Why is Russia having so much difficulty with agriculture? Simply because nature isn't cooperating. (Remember, God said, "I am against you, Russia!") The upheaval of nature in Russia has been extremely severe through the years, especially within the past three or four years. Her supply of food has been affected drastically. She is being hard pressed to see that all her people are properly fed.

As a solution she is turning to the United States — "the breadbasket of the world." Russia is presently buying millions of metric tons of grain from us in order to stave off hunger among her millions. Other than in Moscow, bread lines can now be found throughout Russia. It is amazing how our lands continue to produce bumper crops. We must give praise and glory to God, Who has blessed our nation with such abundance!

No doubt, Russia is in trouble — agriculturally, socially, industrially, militarily, economically. Why? Because God said, "Russia, I'm against you!"

4
A Cloud to Cover
the Land

4
A Cloud to Cover
the Land

In Ezekiel 38:16 God states: *And thou shalt come up against my people of Israel,* **as a cloud to cover the land;** *it shall be in the latter days, and I will bring thee against my land.*

Interpretation must remain consistent; therefore, the use of modern names to identify nations must be applied, as well, to weapons of war and modes of transportation. Today's armies do not use shields, helmets, bows, and arrows; nor do they travel on horseback.

Only modern weapons could produce the kind of fire power

described by Ezekiel. Furthermore, the quick lightninglike thrust of Russian armies would have to rely on aircraft and fast, armored vehicles such as tanks.

This prophecy allows us to see the use of airplanes in modern warfare. As Ezekiel says, Russia shall ascend and be like a storm and come *as a cloud to cover the land.* This is an excellent description of airborne forces, with which Russia is well equipped.

It is Russia who first developed *rapid deployment forces.* Using the rapid deployment techniques, Russia took Ethiopia in November, 1977, and Afghanistan in December, 1979.

God's Double Action

The action that God has pronounced against Russia and its leaders in Ezekiel 38:4 is that Russia shall be turned back and, with hooks in her jaws, be brought into a particular place. This seems to be a double action in relation to Russia.

However, when we consider Russia, we have to consider the two outstanding forces of this nation, the first being her great *political ideology*, which we know as Communism. The other force of this great nation is her very outstanding *military machine*.

In verse four the Lord speaks to Ezekiel and informs him that He will turn back Russia and put hooks in her jaws and bring her forth. He begins immediately talking about her vast army and her allies.

The verse speaks of *all thine army, horses and horsemen, all of them clothed with all sorts of armour, even a great company with bucklers and shields, all of them handling swords.* Again, let me point out that Russia *does not* fight on horseback, neither with shields and swords. We must realize that Ezekiel was using terminology to describe armies of his day.

Russian Satellite Nations

In verse five, Ezekiel begins setting forth the satellite nations of Russia. The identity of these nations furthers our understanding that God is speaking through Ezekiel against Russia.

The first satellite nation is Persia, which in Ezekiel's time was made up of Iraq, Iran, and Afghanistan. These latter day nations are either already within the Russian alliance or seriously leaning toward Russia at this time.

The next satellite is Ethiopia. Ancient Ethiopia, still existing today, covered a large part of the continent of Africa to the south of Egypt. The death of King Haile Selassie, plus governmental and student unrest in Ethiopia, have turned this pro-Western nation to an alliance with Russia.

Libya, in northern Africa on the Mediterranean Sea, is next, having very close ties to Russia due to military treaties of the early fifties.

The Satellite of Gomer

Examining ancient biblical maps, particularly the maps that show the descendants of Noah, we find that Gomer lies in eastern Europe, particularly the area we now know as East Germany, Poland, Hungary, and Czechoslovakia.

It is no coincidence that Germany was divided at the close of World War II. This became necessary in order that there might be a satellite of Russia in that part of the world to fulfill this passage of Scripture. By the *authority* of the Word of God, one realizes that Germany is not going to be united before the battle described in these verses.

The next area mentioned by Ezekiel is Togarmah. The province of Togarmah is south of Meshech, or Moscow, covering much of the highly industrialized area of the nation of Russia, plus Rumania, Bulgaria, and

Turkey. Notice that the Scriptures clearly indicate that all of these satellites of Russia will bring their armies together with the great Russian army to do battle against Israel. These armies will have been well equipped.

Forceful Resistance to Change

Russia, according to verse seven, will have supplied *much* military equipment, and will also have guarded them very closely.

We are aware that on every occasion in which a Russian satellite nation has attempted to change its status, Russia has prevented it from doing so, often with *strong* military resistance to its desire for freedom. Hungary, Czechoslovakia, and Poland are sterling examples of Russia's control and brutality. This information clearly identifies the nation of Ezekiel's prophecy — Russia.

Some years ago, I was observing a Russian military parade and listening to commentary by a leading American newsman. His statement was that he had "seen tanks as though they were great herds of horses." This immediately rang a bell within my spirit, and I recalled the statement found in Ezekiel 38:4,5.

The world is aware that of all Russia's military hardware in her arsenal, the tank — a mechanized horse — is her prize possession. There is a reason for this: The Russians are basically horsemen. At one time Russian cossacks were believed to be the finest military horsemen in the world. It is no secret that Russia produces some of the world's finest horses. Being lovers of horses, Russians would, consequently, be very proud of the military vehicle that has replaced the horse.

5
Russia, Egypt, and
The Suez Canal

5

Russia, Egypt, and The Suez Canal

God said, *I will turn thee back, and . . .
I will bring thee forth*. These events came
almost simultaneously. Prior to 1956,
Russia had not been involved in the
Middle East.

You may recall 1956 as the year that
Egypt, under the leadership of Gamal
Abdel Nasser, seized control of the
Suez Canal from England and France.
The British and French reacted
immediately to retake the canal by
military force, if need be.

Russia, observing these events,
immediately offered aid to Egypt. Her
statement to England and France was

that they should take no action against Egypt; that, if they did, she (Russia) would enter into the conflict.

For the first time since the end of World War II, the United States found herself having to take sides with Russia and to ask England and France to take no military action concerning the Suez Canal.

This was the first occasion for Russia to become committed to the Middle East. Her commitment was that she would stand by Egypt and other Arab nations against any aggressors. "Hooks" had been put into her "jaws," and she had been drawn militarily into the Middle East.

Summer of 1956

In recalling the details of the summer of 1956 and the Suez event, you will discover that Israel moved militarily against Egypt. Through this military action, England and France were to attempt to secure the Suez Canal.

How did all of this come about?

Victory Without Gunfire

Let me take you back a few years in history to the year of 1917 during World War I. A British general by the name of Allenby led an allied force into the Holy Land against the Turks. Miraculously he captured the Holy Land and took Jerusalem without firing a shot. The Turks, who were valiant fighters, fled their Jerusalem entrenchments without resistance. The name *Allenby* had struck fear in the hearts of the Turks, for in their language it means ''a man sent from God.''

Return of God's People

The war came to its close with Britain serving as the protector of the land of Palestine, formerly known as Israel. Because of this development, a group of Jewish men working closely with Parliament came before that governmental body and asked them a

63

favor. The favor was that Britain would permit the Jews to return to their homeland. Out of these conferences came the Balfour Agreement which set aside an area of the land of Palestine for all Jews who wished to return.

However, the majority of the Jews did not want to return. They had become influential and often controlled much wealth in Europe. They were hated, spat upon, and often found it unsafe to walk down the streets. For security they lived behind barred windows and locked gates. Yet they were among the masters in Europe.

There was no incentive for them to return to the land of their fathers. Though the land had once flowed with milk and honey and was fruitful and rich, it had become a desert wilderness, almost totally unprofitable — declared by a British agriculturist to be almost uninhabitable.

God, through His prophets, had pleaded with Israel to return to Him and to their land. Many of the prophets prophesied that this would be done. History records Israel rejecting an opportunity to do so at the end of World War I with the exception of Zionist activity to restore small land areas.

Because the British had granted this favor to the Jews, they were in a position to ask a return favor of the young nation of Israel in 1956. So it was that they called upon the Prime Minister David BenGurion who, we understand, had been one of the young Jewish men to go before Parliament and effect the Balfour Agreement. BenGurion was asked for a favor, and a favor he granted. The agreement was that Israel would use her military might against Egypt for the seizing of the Suez Canal. This, Israel was ready to do.

She had won her war of independence against the Arabs in 1948 and had become a nation on May 15, 1948. From that time until 1956, there had been many armed clashes between the nation of Israel and her Arab neighbors.

Israel's First Military Conflict

Now Israel was ready to try her military strength against her strongest opponent, Egypt. You will recall the story.

Israeli forces moved through the Gaza strip and the Sinai Peninsula and quickly defeated the Egyptian forces driving them back to the Suez Canal. When Israel was in the heat of its attack, Britain and France issued an ultimatum. The ultimatum said that unless both Israel and Egypt ceased firing within twelve hours, Britain and France would attack them both for the protection of the Suez Canal.

Of course, that twelve-hour period expired and the fight continued. British and French navies, paratroopers, fighters, and bombers went into action. The amazing thing we discovered through this military action was that the British and the French are extremely poor marksmen. All of their shells, bombs, and paratroopers fell upon the Egyptians. Not one Israeli was wounded by the British and French attack.

Immediately, the world knew that this whole military action was a preconceived plan by Britain, France, and Israel. When this action began, Russia roared out of her northern quarters, ready to dispatch military force to Egypt. This action had "hooked" the Russian military and drawn them into the Middle East.

Death Blow to Communism

Although these events produced the beginning of the role of Russia in the Middle East, Russia was hindered from coming very forcibly to Egypt's aid by an uprising in Europe. A group of freedom fighters in Hungary had risen up and were overthrowing the Russian occupational forces. In order to put down this rebellion, Russia sent twelve divisions of tanks to Hungary. They slaughtered Hungarians until blood ran in the gutters of the streets of Budapest.

This action by Russia proved to the world the brutal viciousness of Communism. Immediately, Communism lost face in many areas of the world and has not since regained its influence. Actually, this brutal massacre was allowed by God to seriously hinder the rapid advance of Communism, and to strike what would eventually become a death blow to Communism. Therefore, God began the process of "turning Russia back."

So, we see that God allowed two events: one that *turned back* the political ideology of Communism, and the other that *brought* the Russian military machine into the Middle East where it will be utterly destroyed.

6
Land of Unwalled
Villages

6
Land of Unwalled Villages

Verse eight continues by saying, *In the latter years thou shalt come into the land that is brought back from the sword, and is gathered out of many people, against the mountains of Israel, which have been always waste.*

This refers, of course, to the nation of Israel, the nation that was born out of the destruction of World War II. Therefore, this prophecy declares that in latter days, Russia will come against Israel with all of her satellite armies like a cloud to cover the land.

They shall think evil thoughts, such as, ''I will go up to the land of unwalled villages. I will go to them that are at rest dwelling safely with windows, having neither bars nor gates, to take a spoil, and to take a prey; and to turn my hand upon the desolate places that are now inhabited, and upon the people that are gathered out of all nations, and have prospered in the midst of that land.'' (v. 11.)

Notice that Russia makes *no* move against Israel until Israel is at *rest*, indicating peace would come to the Middle East. Verses eleven and fourteen also indicate an era of peace between Israel and her immediate neighbors: Egypt, Saudi Arabia, Jordan, Syria, and Lebanon.

Israel's Ally — The United States

Verse thirteen reveals that Israel has some committed allies and they too recognize Russia's desires to conquer Israel and control the Middle East:

Sheba, and Dedan, and the merchants of Tarshish, with all the young lions thereof, shall say unto thee, Art thou come to take a spoil? hast thou gathered thy company to take a prey? to carry away silver and gold, to take away cattle and goods, to take a great spoil?

These allies, Sheba and Dedan, represent a few Arab nations that are sympathetic toward the nation of Israel, quite likely the ones at peace with Israel.

The major allies of Israel are found by examination of the Merchant of Tarshish and the young lions thereof. The Merchants of Tarshish receive their name from the ancient city of Tarshish on the Mediterranean Sea, where they once traded their goods. These merchantmen represented all of the nations that would one day become the Roman Empire, whose existence would fade away with the total collapse of the Roman Empire.

The Sign of the Lion

Out of the Merchants of Tarshish came the Colonial Empires. The most successful of these was Great Britain. As you know, the symbol of Great Britain is a lion. That symbol exists to this day and no other empire had more young lions than Great Britain. The present young lions are: Canada, Australia, New Zealand, South Africa, and the United States. The mightiest of these young lions now leads the pack; none other than the United States. It is always the strongest young lion who is the leader; the old lion takes his place in the pack.

So it is that among the allies of Israel we find all of the nations of western Europe plus the young lions under the leadership of the United States. Our statement to Russia is, "You have come to take a spoil, to carry away silver and gold, cattle and goods, and we are ready to defend Israel."

Some of you may recall that Israel got an agreement from us in 1956, because of the Suez event. When the conflict over Suez had ended, once more our nation, with Russia, asked Britain, France, and Israel to withdraw their forces and return all holdings to Egypt.

This was not done until Israel received from our nation the agreement they wanted. This agreement was effected between Tel Aviv and Washington, D.C. by President Dwight Eisenhower and Prime Minister David BenGurion. The Israeli ambassador to Washington was Mrs. Golda Meir. She flew back and forth between the two capitals until the agreement was satisfactory to Israel. The American liaison was Vice-president Richard Nixon.

When the agreement was reached, the Israeli forces withdrew and the Gaza strip and Sinai territories were returned to Egypt until the 1967 war.

Twice since the agreement the United States has moved naval and military equipment rapidly to the aid of Israel and her neighbors, once landing 15,000 marines in Lebanon.

7
The Grand Finale

7
The Grand Finale

At this present time, Israel holds much of the land of Palestine which is rightfully hers. Israel now possesses the city of Jerusalem for the first time in over twenty-five hundred years. These accomplishments came about through the Six-Day War of June, 1967.

This fulfilled a prophecy of Jesus Christ: *Jerusalem shall be trodden down of the Gentiles, until the times of the Gentiles be fulfilled* (Luke 21:24).

The meaning of this for you and me is that the church age is at its *closing*. We must begin to look with keen interest toward the appearing of Jesus Christ, for Jesus said that when we see these things begin to come to pass, we are to *look up* for our *redemption draweth nigh* (v. 28).

Watch and Pray . . .

Jesus also instructs us to watch and pray that we may be accounted worthy to escape the things that are coming on the earth. (v. 36.) While we await His appearing, we must "occupy" (which means take possession of) all that surrounds us. (Luke 19:13.) We are observing God at work in behalf of Israel's restoration. He is keeping His Word.

The defeat of the Arabs by Israel in 1967 has placed Russia at a great disadvantage. She has lost her ability to regain influence in the Middle East by diplomacy. There is left to her only one avenue, and that is *military conquest*.

The Six-Day War of 1967 saw a quick defeat of the best Russian strategy and military hardware. Russia wants revenge! She began planning the prophesied invasion of Israel in the fall of 1967. Out of those massive military maneuvers came their rapid deployment force.

However, Ezekiel 38:8, 11, and 14 reveals that Russia will take no direct action against Israel until an era of peace has come. That peace is now beginning to appear with the first step taken by Egypt and Israel. With peace in the Middle East, Russia will be ready to strike. Verse nine clearly establishes the method of Russia's initial attack: by the air, using her powerful rapid deployment force.

God's Anger

And it shall come to pass at the same time when Gog (Russia) *shall come against the land of Israel, saith the Lord God, that my fury shall come up in my face* (v. 18). God is going to become filled with wrath against Russia as she moves against Israel.

Continuing to read this chapter, we discover that Russia moves down from the North with her vast military machine. They move into the mountains north of Israel, and it is there that God stops them.

Notice that God has said He would call for a sword against Russia from all of His mountains. (v. 21.) Ezekiel is not describing a natural mountain, but using a figure of speech, oft times used in the Scriptures, to designate kingdoms.

This is the occasion for the allies of Israel to rise to her defense. God will allow an earthquake that will shake the mountains down to block the way of the advancing Russian horde.

Plague . . . and a Rain of Fire

God then sends an overflowing rain with much hail which will hinder the movement of heavy mechanized equipment and render useless their air force and sophisticated electronic equipment. Fire and brimstone will begin to rain down on the vast army from heaven. This will be both supernatural and nuclear.

Consider for a moment, the effect of this upheaval of nature: a mighty earthquake, so intense that the whole earth will have tremors. The mountains north of Israel and within Lebanon, Turkey, Iraq, Iran, and Syria will fall.

This information immediately causes us to understand that the center of the earthquake would be much further to the north, inside Russia. Realize that the center of such a mighty earthquake could not be just north of Israel, or all Israel would be devastated. Therefore, the center will be much further north, probably just east of Moscow.

Such an earthquake would crush Russian missiles in their underground silos, exploding them and bringing much destruction to Russia. Also, the heavy rains mixed with hail would cause any missiles that may have been launched to explode over Russian territory. Hail is an almost perfect anti-missile weapon.

The armies of Israel and her allies will also have turned their full power against the great Russian war machine. God's divine intervention will cause Russia's military machine to be of no effect!

In fact, Ezekiel 39:3 declares that the Russian soldiers will be unable to fire their guns or even hold them in their hands because of the *plague* that God sends upon them. There will be utter destruction! God said He would send *fire* upon Russia and among them that dwell carelessly along the coast lines (v. 6), so that only one-sixth of Russia escapes the destruction of this horrible battle. What a battle! Millions killed and a part of the earth left devastated.

The Battle

As the present era of Mid-East peace arrives, Russia begins making ready for a quick deadly strike against Israel. The day for the attack dawns and God beats Russia to the punch! As Russians are making their initial move to launch a devastating blow, God unleashes nature and a plague of illness against them.

The upheaval of nature is such that an earthquake of major intensity rocks the mountains north of Israel all the way through the interior of Russia. The effect on that area is cataclysmic.

Along with the earthquake comes an overflowing rain with hail. Such an action of nature not only hinders the movement of armies, but prevents the use of aircraft and intercontinental ballistic missiles, as described in above paragraphs.

According to Ezekiel 38:9, the Russians plan to come by air and take Israel using their rapid deployment forces. This would be a swift action which would prepare the way for a secondary action by their armored divisions and infantry. Russia will not use her nuclear might as she has no wish to destroy the land, nor be delayed in occupying the area. She will be relying on her nuclear readiness to prevent the United States or anyone else from coming to Israel's aid! God takes care of the whole affair!

Russian Military Personnel Immobilized

Heavy rain and hail have a very serious effect on the use of aircraft and electronic equipment. Hail causes electronic equipment, including radar, to go crazy! The earthquake bottles up the armored and infantry divisions. To insure there are no slipups by nature, God sends a physical pestilence, a strange sickness, to every man involved in the military, and they are unable to handle or fire their weapons. The Russian army, navy, and air force are totally affected.

Let me call to your attention that this upheaval of nature affects only the geographical areas of Russia and her satellite nations. Nature does not react against Israel nor any other part of the earth.

The earthquake is of such intensity that all the earth will be affected by the tremors and all people will know that a major catastrophe has occurred. Since Israel and her supporting nations will not be clobbered by nature, they will unleash their devastating fire power against Russia and all the armies assembled with her!

The War Ends

Notice that God calls on nations to supply a sword, which is an implement of war, to be brought down hard upon Russia.

Israel will use her nuclear warheads, the United States will send her ICBMs on their way to Russian targets. Europe will strike its powerful nuclear blow and in only one single day, the war will begin and end.

The Results

In a twenty-four hour period, the most powerful nation on earth will have met more than her match: *God intervening to save Israel!*

The results will leave Russia totally wiped out. The entire army, navy, and air force will be gone — utterly destroyed. *Five-sixths* of the remaining population of Russia will lie dead due to the horrible nuclear strikes against the cities.

What a price to pay; all because men said, ''There is no God,'' and attempted to destroy the people of God, Israel. May I add that some manuscripts point out that no one in Russia will be spared; all will be killed.

This Is Not Armageddon

This is the story of World War III. It is *not* the battle of Armageddon. *Do not* confuse these two battles. They are separate affairs. Take note that the battle discussed in this book is fought in the mountains of Israel far to the north of Jerusalem, between Russia and her satellites and Israel and her allies. The *victor* is Israel. The *defeated foe* is Russia.

It will take Israel seven months to bury the Russian dead and seven years to use up the fuel supplies brought by Russia into the field of battle. This seven-year period is significant in that it is the same amount of time given in the Scriptures to the Tribulation Period, and it is also the period of time that separates the fulfillment of Ezekiel 38 and 39 from the battle of Armageddon.

Armageddon takes place on the final day of the Tribulation Period. So that you may be able to distinguish between these two battles, let me point out that

Scripture says the battle of Armageddon is fought in the plains of Megiddo, outside of Jerusalem. The battle of Armageddon is fought between the Antichrist and his armies and the Lord Jesus Christ and His heavenly host.

Of course, we know who wins this battle — Jesus Christ.

Differences Between the Two Battles

After Armageddon, Jesus sets up a kingdom here on the earth for a thousand years. So there are marked differences between the two battles.

The first battle and the outcome of ''God's Conquest of Russia'' is necessary in order that the way may be fully prepared for the release of the Antichrist. When he comes, he will not come as the Antichrist, or even declaring himself to be God, but will come as a diplomatic strongman with religious sympathy to Israel.

The anti-God nation of Russia would be a hindering factor to the Antichrist. Therefore, in God's conquest of Russia, this hindering factor is removed. However, Russia is *not* the withholding force of 2 Thessalonians 2. The withholder of the Antichrist in that reference is the Holy Spirit-energized *Church of Jesus Christ!*

The Dead in Christ Raised Up

Just before the time of World War III, the Lord Jesus Christ descends from heaven with a shout. The dead in Christ are raised, and the living saints are caught up to meet the Lord in the air (1 Thess. 4:16,17), therefore removing all hindrance to the revealing of the man who is to become the Antichrist. We are on the threshold of the appearing of Jesus Christ, at which time He will receive His own unto Himself.

The prophesied event of World War III is at the very beginning of the Tribulation some seven years before Armageddon.

Let me close this book urging you to prepare yourself for the event of the appearing of Jesus Christ!

The events of this prophecy, and the beginning of the fulfillment thereof, greatly aid our understanding of the timetable of the Church and the soon-appearing of Jesus Christ. Additional understanding through prophetic events is also cast upon the books of Daniel and Revelation.

God Is Obligated To His Word

Since God is obligated to His Word, He *must* defend and protect Israel. That covenant is an everlasting one; therefore, God has no alternative but to allow the action just described. God is just, and He will not bring about the destruction of Russia without first giving her every opportunity to repent. Remember, God is slow to anger, but He will not acquit the wicked.

Pray for the Russian People

The Church in America should place the people of Russia in their prayers. We should pray earnestly that God, through the Holy Spirit, will energize and divinely protect the Church in Russia. We should use our faith to believe that God will bring the Church from its "underground" base to the people, in order that a great harvest can take place.

Think about this: Every Russian that you and I can pray into the Kingdom of God will be one less to have to face this terrible event revealed by Ezekiel. The Church company in Russia has just as much right to "escape all these things that shall come to pass" as do Christians at any other place on the earth. *Pray the prayer of faith for all Russian people.*

Hilton Sutton is regarded by many as the nation's foremost authority on Bible prophecy as related to current events and world affairs.

As an ordained minister of the Gospel, Rev. Sutton served as pastor for several years before being led out into the evangelistic field. Today he travels throughout the world, teaching and preaching the Word. He takes the words of the most accurate news report ever — the Word of God — and relates it to the news today.

Having spent over twenty years researching and studying the book of Revelation, Hilton Sutton explains Bible prophecy and world affairs to the people in a way that is clear, concise, and easy to understand. He presents his messages on a layman's level and shows the Bible to be the most accurate, up-to-date book ever written.

Hilton Sutton and his family make their home in Humble, Texas, where he serves as chairman of the board of Mission To America, a Christian organization dedicated to carrying the Gospel of Jesus Christ to the world.